In Plain and Simple English

BookCaps™ Study Guides
www.bookcaps.com

© 2012. All Rights Reserved.

Table of Contents

Introduction

Mormonism is the religion of members of The Church of Jesus Christ of Latter-Day Saints, who are known as Mormons after one of their holy books. It is a Christian religion which its devotees believe is a re-establishment of the Christian church as Jesus intended it to be. Mormons believe that other Christian churches have gone astray from Jesus' intentions.

Mormonism began in the 1820s, in the United States. It was founded by Joseph Smith, who claimed that when he was unsure which branch of Christianity to follow he had received a vision from God and Jesus who told him that he should follow none but form his own church. Three years after this he was visited by an angel named Moroni who told him where to find golden plates inscribed with holy text. He dug these up and translated them, and they are what forms the Book of Mormon.

After the murder of Smith by a mob in 1844 Brigham Young, one of his followers, decided that the Mormons could no longer stand the persecution they faced on the East Coast of America. In 1847, he and 16,000 followers began a great trek westwards until they came to Utah, where they established Salt Lake City, which remains the headquarters of the church to this day.

Mormon beliefs have much in common with other Christian religions, and the Bible is their principle holy book (alongside the Book of Mormon). However, there are also many important differences in their views with regard to issues such as the Trinity, the nature of God and the nature of life after death.

Mormons worship in chapels and in a special church called The Temple. Chapel services are for regular worship and broadly follow many other Christian rites, including the taking of Holy Communion, hymn singing and prayers. The Temple is only used for special services and, unlike chapel services, only Mormons are permitted to attend.

Mormons have a very strong sense of the importance of family life, and they are essentially conservative on matters such as sex outside marriage, tobacco and alcohol. Missionary work plays an important part in the faith, and there are over fifty thousand currently serving. Over the course of the history of the church, over a million Mormons have served as missionaries.

There are currently around fourteen million devotees of Mormonism in the world, of whom just under half live in the United States. Twelve percent of these (around 1.7 million) still live in Utah, where they comprise sixty percent of the state's population.

Mormons have suffered a great deal of persecution throughout the history of their church. This has sometimes been caused by religious and political differences and sometimes by ignorance as to the truth about Mormonism.

Chapter 1: History of Mormonism

At the beginning of the nineteenth century in America, a religious movement flourished which became known as the Second Great Awakening. This movement was in many ways a reaction against the Enlightenment of eighteenth century Europe, with its emphasis on the secular, science and reasoning which were often set above the traditional Christian churches.

One element of the Second Great Awakening which distinguished it from more traditional churches was its belief in the ability of men to receive gifts of prophecy and visions from God. In traditional Christian theology, this form of communication from God ended with the Apostles (though it was granted to some of the saints). Many men claimed to have experienced such visions, including Joseph Smith Snr, the father of the founder of the Church of Jesus Christ of Latter Day Saints (LDS).

Joseph Smith Jnr was born in Sharon, Vermont on December 23rd 1805. When Smith was around twelve, his family moved to Palmyra in the western part of New York state, an area in which the Second Great Awakening and its Revivalist meetings were very active. Smith grew up in an atmosphere in which the concept of God's giving instruction to His followers on earth was well accepted, as was the idea that new forms of religion were required to return Christian religion to the true path after the apostasy (diversion from true faith, see **The Great Apostasy**, below) of the traditional churches.

According to Smith's later accounts, in around 1820 he went into woods near Manchester, NY (where the family had acquired a farm) to pray for guidance as to which church he should join. He suddenly felt as if he was about to be overwhelmed by evil, but God and Jesus Christ appeared to save him. He was told that his sins were forgiven him, and also that he should not join any established church as they were all in error. He was further told that at some future date the "fullness of the Gospel" would be made clear to him.

In 1823, Smith was praying for forgiveness when he claimed to receive a visit from an angel named Moroni, who told him that, on a hill near his home, there were buried golden plates on which were inscribed the history of an early American people. Smith went to the location and tried to take the plates, but he was prevented by the angel.

Over the next few years, Smith travelled in New York State and Pennsylvania, working as a farmhand and as a treasure seeker. Treasure seeking was an accepted (by some) profession at that time, with practitioners claiming to be able to find precious buried objects through the use of divining rods and "seeing stones". It was not universally accepted, as can be seen from the fact that Smith was prosecuted in 1826 for falsely claiming he could find treasure.

During these times, Smith made an annual visit to the hill where the golden plates were buried, but the angel always prevented him from removing them. At the beginning of 1827, Smith eloped with (as her parents objected to his profession of treasure seeking) and married Emma Hale, whom he had met in her parents' boarding house, in Pennsylvania.

On September 22nd that year Smith, who was back living on his parents' farm, made another of his annual visits to the hill, taking Emma with him. This time he was allowed to take away the plates. He said that the angel had told him that he was not to show them to anyone else, but to make a translation of them.

Smith had been a member of a treasure seeking company, and although he had resigned from it the other members felt that he had deceived them and was keeping the golden plates to himself when they should have been shared equally. The unpleasantness caused by this was such that near the end of 1827 Smith moved with his wife back to her hometown of Harmony, Pennsylvania.

Living with financial assistance from a neighbor from Palmyra, Martin Harris, Smith began his work of translating the plates, for which he claimed to use a seeing stone given to him by Moroni. The translations were dictated to Emma. Early in 1828 Harris joined the Smiths to assist with the translation. Harris took a copy of some of the characters from the plates which Smith had made to a prominent classical scholar named Charles Anthon. Harris claimed that Anthon authenticated the characters as genuine Egyptian hieroglyphs and only withdrew his authentication when he was told they came from an angel, though Anthon always insisted he had seen that they were a hoax from the start and never gave them any credence.

By mid-1828, Harris was beginning to have his doubts about the authenticity of the plates and is also thought to have been under pressure from his wife to stop spending their money on Smith. He asked Smith if he could take the translation to show family members but lost it (it was the only copy). Smith said that this event caused him to lose his ability to translate, but he regained it on September 22nd and began again.

In April 1829, Smith met Oliver Cowdrey, who became his scribe with the two working together in Fayette, NY. They accomplished a great deal of the translation very quickly. Amongst other things they found in the translation was an instruction that a new church should be founded and that it should have baptism at its heart; when they read this the two men baptized each other. Later, in 1829, (they later claimed) both men were visited by an angel who gave them instructions as to the construction of their new religion, including that they should have a priesthood; Smith and Cowdrey both became priests. The Book of Mormon was published in March 1830, again funded by Martin Harris.

Smith and Cowdrey had been baptizing followers from 1829, but there was no formal church establishment until April 6th 1830, when the Church of Christ was founded. The church remained relatively small, but gained much attention through the publication of The Book of Mormon. There was some hostility to the church, much of it from those who remembered Smith's earlier behavior as a treasure seeker. The disturbances became so grave that Smith was arrested and brought to trial in Colesville, NY, on a charge of creating public disorder. Although he was acquitted, he had to escape from a mob, which had gathered to witness the trial.

In the face of such opposition, Smith decided that the Church had to find a new home, which would become the New Jerusalem. He sent Cowdrey on a mission to Missouri to find the location of the city, with instructions that he should convert Native Americans, as well. Cowdrey's journey took him through Kirtland, Ohio where he encountered Oliver Rigdon and his hundred strong Disciples of Christ organization. Rigdon and his followers quickly decided to join the Church of Christ, and after meeting with Smith in New York Rigdon was appointed as his second in command. As opposition to Smith grew in New York, he announced that Kirtland was on the boundary of the New Jerusalem, and that his followers should gather there. He himself moved there in January 1831.

Smith began to form the shape of the church, establishing foundations which are still a part of the LDS today. He created the United Order of Enoch, a communal system, but later in 1831, in response to the demands of elders of the church, he created a higher order of the priesthood, the Melchizedek order.

Meanwhile, Cowdrey announced that he had discovered the site of the New Jerusalem in Jackson County, Missouri. After visiting the site Smith agreed that it was correct, but Rigdon objected, and, throughout the first part of the 1830s, the Church remained split between Jackson County and Kirtland.

There were problems for the Church in both areas. In Kirtland former members of the Church who had grown disaffected with Smith's power tarred and feathered him and Rigdon, beating them unconscious in the process. Meanwhile, the settlers in Missouri came under attack from native inhabitants who objected both to their religion and the disturbance they caused to the balance of political power in the area. When the settlers tried to defend themselves they were driven from the county.

Smith led an expedition to try to reclaim Jackson County, which was called "Zion's Camp". The expedition was a failure as Smith's forces were outnumbered, had no official support and were ravaged by cholera. Smith announced that he had a vision that the Church was unworthy to regain Zion due to the failure of the United Order, and he reorganized the structure of the Church and renamed it the Church of Latter Day Saints. A great Temple was built in Kirtland which was endowed in 1836.

This Temple was a source of great trouble for Smith, as the Church had borrowed heavily to finance the construction. To try and stabilize the debt problem, Smith created the Kirtland Safety Society in 1837, a bank organization which issued banknotes. Smith invested heavily himself and encouraged his followers to do so, but it collapsed within a month. Many of his followers lost large sums and left the Church, blaming Smith. At the start of 1838 a warrant was issued for Smith's arrest on a charge of bank fraud, and he and Rigdon had to flee to Missouri.

The Missouri branch of the Church had established a new town named Far West, and Smith gave up his ambition of reclaiming Jackson County, declaring instead that Far West was the New Zion. At the same time, he gave his church another new name, The Church of Jesus Christ of Latter Day Saints. Shortly afterwards many of the members of the Church from Kirtland joined Smith. Smith led a major restructuring of the Church, expelling many members who opposed him; even his early associate Cowdrey was put on trial for financial misdemeanors and accusing Smith of adultery. At the same time, a secret organization called the Danites was formed, which harassed and drove out those who opposed Smith.

As in Jackson County the resident Missourians objected to the presence of the Church. On August 6th 1838, residents attempted to stop members of the Church from voting in elections, and violence swiftly escalated into the 1838 Mormon War. Farms belonging to members of the Church were burned and looted, whilst Mormon forces did the same to non-believers. The war came to an end in November, when Church forces fought a battle with the Missouri state militia and the state Governor ordered that Mormons should be driven from the state. The Mormons surrendered, and Smith was court-martialed for treason, which would have led to him being executed. However, he successfully argued that he was a civilian and so was imprisoned to await a civil trial.

While Smith was in prison one of the most important figures in Mormon history, Brigham Young, came to the fore. He lead an expedition of fourteen thousand Mormons into Illinois to establish a new settlement, and when Smith managed to join him after escaping from custody in 1839 they established a new city which they named Nauvoo (Hebrew for "beautiful"). Due to the influence of highly placed converts to Mormonism the city was given a powerful charter which enabled Smith to resist attempts to have him extradited to Missouri to stand trial. Another part of the charter allowed Nauvoo to raise its own militia, with Smith as its Lieutenant General.

During this period, Smith continued to develop the concept of the LDS, introducing many key features such as the baptism of the dead and the Relief Society for women, who were not permitted to join the priesthood. He also announced that he had received a vision that Zion was not going to be confined to a small territory but was to cover all of North and South America. Brigham Young and other prominent Mormons were sent on missionary expeditions to Europe, where they made a significant number of converts amongst the poor.

In May 1842, an assassination attempt was made on the Governor of Missouri for which Smith's personal bodyguard was charged (though later acquitted), and there were rumors that Smith had prophesied the Governor's death. An attempt was made to extradite him to Missouri, but it failed when it was declared unconstitutional. A second attempt was made on the grounds of his previous treason indictment, but that also failed. Although Smith was safe for a time, political opinion in Illinois was turning against him.

Late in 1843 Smith issued demands that Nauvoo should become an independent territory with the right to use troops to defend itself. He wrote to the presidential candidates in the forthcoming election and asked what they would do to defend the Mormons: when he received non-committal answers he declared himself a candidate for the presidency.

Smith's downfall came about in 1844 as a result of disagreement within the Church. Smith fell out with some of his closest allies over matters concerning the economy of Nauvoo, and two of them accused him of proposing marriage to their wives (Smith had begun to consider promoting polygamy in the Church from 1841 and had been practicing it himself, possibly from as early as 1837). His opponents formed a breakaway faction and succeeded in having Smith indicted for polygamy. The opponents also launched a newspaper, the Nauvoo Expositor, which denounced polygamy and accused Smith of wanting to become a king. The city council, under Smith's influence, ordered the Nauvoo Legion (the city militia) to destroy the Expositor's presses. This caused public outrage, and Smith, fearing an uprising, raised the militia to its full available strength. In response to this, the Governor of Illinois threatened to raise a larger militia and fight unless Smith surrendered. Smith fled at first but then returned and surrendered.

Smith, alongside his bother Hyrum, was taken to the nearby town of Carthage and charged with inciting a riot: the charge was later upgraded to that of treason against the State of Illinois. On June 27th 1844, the Carthage jail was stormed by a mob. Hyrum Smith was killed instantly, and Joseph Smith, despite attempting to defend himself with a pistol, which had been smuggled in to him, was shot many times and fell from a window. Nobody was ever successfully prosecuted for his murder.

Smith's death led to a great deal of infighting as to who should succeed him as leader of the LDS. Hyrum Smith was the natural successor, but he had died with Smith, and their younger brother Samuel died (amidst unproven accusations of foul play) before he could press his claim. Sidney Rigdon, the last surviving member of the First Presidency of the Church, who had been chosen as Smith's running mate for the Presidency of the USA, claimed he had received a vision instructing him to assume leadership. Meanwhile, Emma Smith, Joseph's widow, favored William Marks, stake president of Nauvoo, but he preferred Rigdon's claim. Brigham Young, as the most senior of the Twelve Apostles (the highest ruling body in the Church below the Presidency) also pressed his claim.

On August 8th 1844, a conference was held in Nauvoo to decide the issue of the leadership, which developed into a straight fight between Rigdon and Young. According to witnesses Young miraculously assumed the voice and appearance of Joseph Smith during his speech, and he was acclaimed leader by the church members present. Rigdon, claiming to be in fear for his life, fled to Pittsburgh with his followers and established the Church of Christ (reverting to LDS' original name). He and his followers were excommunicated from the LDS, and in turn, Young and his followers were excommunicated from the Church of Christ.

Various other groups also split from the mainstream of the LDS (see **Branches of Mormonism**, below), but Young's group was, and remains, by far the largest. The events of 1844 had hardened the attitudes of the non-Mormon population of Illinois against the Church, and a period of persecution followed. In 1846, Young took the decision that his people could no longer tolerate the persecution and led the Trek West in search of land which nobody else wanted where the Church could establish itself in peace. The pioneers, numbering around fourteen thousand, suffered great hardship due to poor weather and their own poor planning and provisioning. However, after wintering in Nebraska in 1846/47 they reached Salt Lake Valley, Utah, in summer 1847 and Salt Lake City was established, which became and remains the world headquarters of the LDS.

Although the intention of Young was to form a Mormon territory beyond governmental control, Utah was quickly incorporated into US territory (although it did not join the Union until 1896). However, it retained (and does to this day) its uniquely Mormon character, with 60% of Utah residents being Mormons. This was made possible due to large scale immigration of the Mormons who had stayed in Nauvoo, Mormons from other areas of the USA and ultimately from Europe.

Many tensions still existed between the new settlers and the US Government, which culminated in the Utah War of 1857/8. In the 1856 Presidential election polygamy had become a major issue, and Mormons also claimed that the President was seeking a distraction from the pressing issue of slavery. Alleging that the Mormons were rebelling against the government President Buchanan sent a US army force to Utah. The Mormons responded with a guerilla campaign (no proper battles were fought during the "war") of harassing the US forces and other settlers on their way to California. In the most notorious incident, the Mountain Meadows massacre, 120 travelers to California, including women and children, were murdered. The Mormons originally blamed the attack on Native Americans and the motives for it are unclear.

Despite this attack and others, only around 150 people (including the Mountain Meadows victims) were killed in the Utah War. Eventually a negotiated settlement was reached, with a full pardon being given to all Mormon participants and Brigham Young agreeing to give up his role as Governor of Utah and pass it to a non-Mormon.

On Young's death in 1877, the succession passed, as it had to him, to the most senior of the Twelve Apostles. This became the established rule and has continued, with exceptions, to this day.

Throughout the 20th and 21st centuries, Mormonism has continued to grow and spread, but its essential creed and practices have remained as they were under the rule of Smith and Young. However, polygamy was abolished in 1904, which removed a prime cause for distrust of the Church amongst outsiders. With the advent of radio, the weekly performances of the Mormon Tabernacle Choir helped spread knowledge and acceptance of Mormonism. As global travel became more available and affordable the LDS has branched out through missionary work into all parts of the world, so that today more than half of the estimated fourteen million members of the Church live outside the USA.

Chapter 2: Theology

Mormon theology has the same roots as other Christian religions, in that at its heart is a belief in God the Father, Jesus the Son and the Holy Spirit. This belief is stated explicitly in the very first of the thirteen Mormon Articles of Faith. However, as we shall see, Mormon theology has evolved in some ways very different to the mainstream of Christian faith, filtered through their specific beliefs and the instructions in their other holy books.

The Godhead

The first Article of Faith states, "We believe in God the Eternal Father…" God to Mormons is a literal father, which they deduce through the Biblical verse Hebrews 12:9, "We have had fathers of our flesh…" Mormons believe that prior to our lives on earth we lived in heaven with God as spirits. Mankind has been created in the image of God, i.e. God has a physical body of flesh and bones. However, he does not have blood. This contrasts with other Christian religions who believe that only Jesus assumed a physical body.

Mormons view God as the creator (through Jesus) of all things, and that he is omniscient (all-knowing), omnipresent (existing everywhere and at all times) and omnipotent (all-powerful). It is possible for a human being to see God, but only if they are without sin and when they are in a state of grace. The Mormon names for God are Elohim, Creator, Supreme Being, Supreme Governor and Father of Mankind.

Jesus Christ is an essential figure in the beliefs of Mormons, although there are important differences between their view of him and those of other Christian faiths. Although our spirits are all children of God, only Jesus is God's physical child, who was born of the Virgin Mary. Mormons believe that Jesus, in his heavenly form, created the earth, the universe and all living things under the direction of his Father. They believe in the Biblical account that Jesus was crucified, died and was resurrected to atone for the sins of all mankind. After Jesus rose from the dead he appeared to the Nephites, who Mormons believe are a tribe of Israel who migrated to America in 600BC. The only way mankind can achieve salvation is through following the perfect example of Jesus. Mormons have over two hundred names for Jesus, drawn from the Bible, the Holy Books of Mormonism and revelations received by members of the faith.

The Holy Ghost is the third member of the Godhead. Unlike God and Jesus, the Holy Ghost has no physical body, which allows it to enter into the hearts of human beings and testify to the truth of the existence of the other two parts of the Godhead. The Holy Ghost is present at baptism to cleanse humans' sins and comes to humans at times of trouble to bring God's counsel and peace.

It is important to note that one of the main theological differences between Mormonism and other Christian faiths is that Mormons believe that the Father, Son and Holy Ghost are three separate beings. Traditional Christian teaching puts great stress upon the three elements of the Trinity being indivisible elements of the same body, but Mormonism claims that this is a corruption of the truth which arose from the Great Apostasy (see below).

A devout Mormon endeavors, through his actions and observances on earth, to be appointed to the highest level of the Celestial kingdom (see **Heaven and Hell**, below). Those who attain this level become as brothers with Christ and joint-heirs with Him to God. They will then spend eternity learning to become more and more like God Himself. This represents a very different view of mankind's place in heaven to that of other Christian faiths, which teach that mankind in heaven will still be subordinate to God and Christ.

Original Sin

Mormons believe in the Biblical account of the creation of mankind with Adam and Eve in the Garden of Eden. However, they also believe that for Adam and Eve to fall by eating from the Tree of Knowledge was a part of God's plan, and that he had already prepared a Savior for mankind before he created them. Therefore, the concept of Original Sin, that all human beings are born as sinners due to Adam's transgression, does not exist in the Mormon faith. Mormons cite the Book of Deuteronomy (24:16) as their authority: "Every man shall be put to death for his own sin." Every human being will be judged only by his own actions on earth.

Heaven and Hell

Mormons believe that there are four different places men go to when they die, depending on their actions while on earth. These are the Celestial Kingdom, the Terrestrial Kingdom, the Telestial Kingdom and the Outer Darkness.

The Celestial Kingdom is the highest level of heaven, where God and Jesus Christ reside. This is reserved for those who have repented of their sins and received forgiveness through Christ's sacrifice, have kept the commandments and received the Gift of the Holy Ghost (see **Mormon Worship**, below). The Celestial Kingdom has three levels, with the highest reserved for those who have been sealed in marriage. Children who die before they reach the age for baptism go automatically to the Celestial Kingdom.

The Terrestrial Kingdom is occupied by those who were good people in life but did not fully accept God and Jesus, or did not work hard enough to testify their faith. This level also houses those who died without receiving Jesus but did after death (this is why Mormons perform the Baptism of the Dead, see **Mormon Worship**, below). In this Kingdom, the inhabitants see Jesus but they are denied full sight of God.

The Telestial Kingdom is for unrepentant sinners. Before they gain the Telestial kingdom they will suffer much at the hands of Satan to atone for their sins, but they will eventually be granted a place at the last resurrection.

The final element of the afterlife in Mormon belief is the Outer Darkness. This is reserved for "sons of perdition": those who have been given witness of Christ but later denied Him. Cain is an example of a son of perdition, who met Christ but later chose Satan. There is no forgiveness for sons of perdition: they suffer eternally at the hands of Satan.

Repentance

The concept of repentance for sin is very important within the LDS. The Articles of Faith state that repentance is the second most important principle of the Gospels after faith in Jesus Christ. Mormons believe that humans are put on earth to prepare for an eternal life in heaven, and that we cannot avoid sin. These sins are atoned through the sacrifice of Jesus, but only if we truly repent.

Mormons believe that all men sin every day in some way, whether in thought, word or deed or simply through omission (not performing a duty one should have). The LDS teaches that as men sin every day, so they should repent every day. Putting off repentance is strongly discouraged, as there will come a time when it is too late to repent, and things which should have been repented may be forgotten and so held against one in the afterlife.

Mormons should repent of their sins through both prayer and deeds. Through prayer, a Mormon should ask forgiveness from God, but he should also make amends to the person he has wronged through apology and recompense where necessary.

The Great Apostasy

The apostles appointed by Christ are accepted by Mormons as having the authority of Christ and they are revered in the church. However, they believe that, after Jesus' ascension and the death of his directly appointed apostles, the Christian religion fell in apostasy, which means abandoning true principles. As the apostles were martyred there were none left with priestly authority who could prevent early Christians twisting the true doctrine of Christ, and without further guidance by means of revelation pagan beliefs and traditions were allowed to creep back into the church. A prime example which they point to is the decision at the Council of Nicaea (325AD) to accept the belief of the unified Trinity, which Mormons believe is erroneous (see **Godhead**, above). To Mormons, all the early councils of the Christian faith were driven by human politics and were lacking in divine guidance and revelation. They, therefore, reject the theology which was shaped at these meetings.

Mormons believe that due to this apostasy (which they claim is predicted in the Bible and is part of God's plan) God found it necessary to appoint a new messenger to recall Christians from error, which he did in appointing Joseph Smith as a saint. This means that LDS is the only Christian Church which has true priestly authority (that is, authority directly from God) to spread God's message for mankind. Mormons do recognize that other branches of Christianity, and indeed other religions, do good work, but claim they only see a small portion of God's plan due to their errors.

Chapter 3: The Holy Books

The Mormon faith rests on four Holy Books, which are known as the Standard Works and often bound together in a single collection. These are the Bible, The Book of Mormon, The Doctrine and Covenants and The Pearl of Great Price.

Bible study is a very important part of Mormon faith and theology. Mormons accept the Bible as the true word of God, with the caveat that some of the text has been corrupted through human error or alteration to suit particular beliefs. They study both the Old and New Testaments, but they reject the Apocrypha (the extra books included in the Catholic Bible). The Bible used by the LDS is the King James Version, but with footnotes relating the text to the Mormon faith. Some of these footnotes refer to Joseph Smith's translation of the Bible, which is regarded more as an aid to study than a complete version on its own.

The Book of Mormon is the essential text of the LDS. Mormons believe that the text was inscribed on golden plates, the location of which was given to Joseph Smith by the angel Moroni. He dug them up and translated them, and they comprise the book (for more on what is in the book see **The Book of Mormon**, below). Mormons study the Book of Mormon and the Bible together and believe both are the word of God, but they believe that the Book of Mormon is more accurate and complete than the Bible.

The Doctrine and Covenants are a record of the revelations given by God to Joseph Smith from 1823 to his death. They include much information about the history of the LDS and set out the essential foundations of Mormonism. They also include some later additions, inserted when there was a major change in doctrine, for example, the abolition of polygamy in 1890.

The Pearl of Great Price is a collection of other works of Joseph Smith, collected from his pamphlets and letters. It is in five sections. "Selections from the Book of Moses" and "Joseph Smith – Matthew" are Smith's translations of the Bible. "The Book of Abraham" is Smith's translation of some ancient Egyptian papyri which he purchased in 1835. It contains an account of Abraham's journey into Egypt and has many sections which reflect fundamental Mormon beliefs. There is much controversy over this section, as experts claim that the parts of the papyri which survive show that they are simply first century BC funerary texts (scripts buried with the dead) which have no relation to Smith's "translation". This is fiercely disputed by Mormons, who claim variously that the surviving papyri (they were lost for some years) are not the ones from which Smith translated, that apparent errors and inconsistencies are due to their being later copies of original texts or that Smith translated them through divine revelation rather than literally. The other two sections are "Joseph Smith – History", an account of Smith's life up until his vision, and "The Articles of Faith", thirteen statements of fundamental LDS beliefs. These were originally part of a letter written by Smith but were included in the collection later.

These books together form the canon of the Mormon faith. Other beliefs in Mormonism, even if they are generally accepted, are not official doctrine. If a prophet (church leader, see **Church Organization**, below) wishes to add or change anything in the canon, it must be put to the authorities and will only be included after a debate and vote.

The Book of Mormon

The Book of Mormon is the essential text of Mormonism, and is regarded by Mormons as having the same validity and divine authority as the Bible.

Joseph Smith claimed that the Book of Mormon was given to him on engraved gold plates. He was told where to find these plates by Moroni, an angel who in life had been the last author of the Book. Smith described the writing on the plates as being "reformed Egyptian", and a small sample of the alphabet used, drawn by Smith, resembles modified Egyptian hieroglyphs, though not of a type any expert has ever been able to identify.

Along with the plates Smith claimed that God gave him the ability to translate them, which he did between 1827 and 1829. He then said that he had returned the plates to Moroni as he had no further need of them. Smith said that the angel had forbidden him from showing the plates to any other man whilst he was working on the translation: he did supposedly show them to eleven others, whose testimony as to their existence appears at the start of the Book.

The Book is organized into smaller books, and these are divided into chapters and verses. Like much of the Bible, the books are named after their narrators or main characters.

Essentially the Book of Mormon is a narrative history, although it contains many digressions relating to spiritual and doctrinal matters. It tells the story of an Israelite named Lehi, who was guided by God to leave Jerusalem with his family and others just before it fell to the Babylonians in 586BC. This group then sailed across the ocean to America.

The rest of the book details the life of the new civilization in America. The group split into two tribes, the Nephites and the Lamanites, who were often at war with each other.

In the book 3 Nephi, there is an account of the visit of Jesus Christ to America after his resurrection. He preached in much the same way as in the Gospels, including reprising the Sermon on the Mount. As a result of this visit a peaceful society sprang up, but, within a few generations, war had broken out once more.

The actual Book of Mormon, the third from last book, was written by a Nephite leader called Mormon (a Christian) who was charged with keeping the records of the Nephi. It records the battles between the Nephites and the Lamanites and is completed by Mormon's son Moroni after Mormon died in battle.

The Book finishes with the Book of Ether, a record of the Jaredites, a much earlier civilization who had come to America in 2500BC from the Tower of Babel, and the Book of Moroni. The Book of Moroni details the final defeat of the Nephites and the collapse of true religion which followed.

The Book has many political and religious digressions which inspired later Mormon theology, particularly the statement that Adam's fall was a part of God's plan (see **Original Sin**, above). There is also much about America, which is described as the most exceptional of lands. It is stated that a righteous society in America will be under divine protection, but should it become unrighteous it will be destroyed and replaced.

In style the Book resembles the language of the King James Version of the Bible, indeed some experts claim that some phrases are lifted directly from the Bible, though this is either denied by Mormons or explained by stating that it is to be expected as God inspired both books. There have also been claims that other works were also plagiarized for the book.

These plagiarism doubts, as well as the lack of any archaeological evidence in America for the existence of the Nephites or the Lamanites, have led some Mormons to believe that the Book is meant to be read as an allegory and was the work of Joseph Smith, although it was divinely inspired. However, the view of most believers and the official Church doctrine is that the Book of Mormon is a true history.

Chapter 4: Church Organization

The LDS is led by a President, who is also a Prophet. Mormons believe that the Prophet is God's representative on earth and that God speaks through him to the church. The Prophet is in every way equal to biblical prophets such as Abraham and Noah, and his words have equal importance.

Mormons view time as being split into a series of "dispensations". At the start of each dispensation, God appoints a prophet (beginning with Adam) who will be rejected and the world will fall into apostasy, or error. Then God will appoint a new prophet to lead humanity back to the true path. The current dispensation began in 1820 with Joseph Smith and continues through his successors as leaders of the LDS. The Prophet is responsible for making changes to church doctrine and policy, and when he does so this is regarded as being the word of God.

Mormons are often mocked or criticized for investing faith in the Prophet and following his instructions without question. However, they say that the Prophet is guided by Jesus, who would never allow him to spread errors, and so they are really investing their faith in Jesus rather than a man. They also say that when they receive instruction from the prophet they pray over it and receive confirmation from God that it is His word.

It is believed that God appoints new prophets so that each may address the concerns of their own time. Therefore, the most important prophet to a Mormon is the current one, as he is giving God's specific instructions for life today. The Prophet may issue guidance at any time, but he speaks to the whole church at conferences every April and October.

The Prophet presides over a council of twelve apostles and has two or more counselors as his special assistants, usually (though not always) chosen from among the apostles. Each of the apostles is also a prophet and ready to become President, but they do not receive instruction from God unless they become President. When the current President dies or resigns usually the most senior of the apostles takes his place.

Below the apostles are the seventies, a group of elders, so called as in the Gospel of Luke it is mentioned that Jesus had seventy disciples. Most of the seventies are area presidents, having responsibility for the church in a particular country or area. Grouped under the area presidents are stake presidents, leaders of a group of congregations rather like a diocese in other Christian faiths. A district is a still smaller unit and then come individual congregations.

An individual congregation is known as a ward and is led by a bishop. This can seem confusing to other Christians as in their faiths a bishop is responsible for many churches, not just one congregation: the Mormon "bishop" is similar to a rabbi or priest. The bishop is responsible for all matters pertaining to his congregation, including presiding over worship and appointing leaders of different church programs. Unlike in other churches a man may not apply to become a bishop: he is chosen by the stake president from amongst the congregation. He is then confirmed by a vote of confirmation from the congregation (not an election). There is no fixed term of service for a bishop, but he will usually serve for around five years.

There are three other important orders in the LDS: these are Patriarch, High Priest and Elder. Members of these orders are responsible for giving blessings (see **Blessings**, below).

All male Mormons become members of the "priesthood", meaning they have the right to act for God and bring his word to humanity. Those who are born Mormons join the priesthood at age twelve (converts do so upon joining) by receiving the laying on of hands from men already in the priesthood. Initially all males hold the Aaronic priesthood, then once they have proved spiritually and morally worthy (and are over eighteen) they are appointed to the Melchizedek priesthood. Gaining the Melchizedek priesthood is particularly important for adult males as it allows them to give blessings to their wives and families. Women are not permitted to join the priesthood.

Mormon Worship

Great stress is laid in Mormonism on the importance of the family unit. It is seen as vital that the home be a centre of worship. Family members should pray both separately and together as well as engaging in study and discussion of the holy books. Mormons have a tradition of a Family Home Evening, where family members make sure that they are all gathered together to pray, read from the scriptures and affirm their faith once a week. Traditionally this takes place on a Monday, and no other Church activities take place on that day, but it can be moved if, for example, a family member is unavoidably called away on a Monday. The Church sends outreach workers to the homes of members of its congregation once a month to check that all is well and to offer help with any difficulties.

The Sabbath worship takes place in Mormon meeting houses. These are usually quite simple buildings with a chapel, meeting hall, classrooms and offices for church administration. There are no crucifixes in Mormon meeting houses as they believe that one should worship the living Christ: for this reason, there are often depictions of other events from Christ's life.

The Mormon Sabbath is, as in other Christian churches, traditionally on a Sunday. However, in countries where the holy day is different it may be moved so that a Mormon is not disadvantaged, so in Israel Mormons celebrate the Sabbath on a Saturday and in Arabic countries on a Friday.

The Sabbath service contains many elements which are common to all Christian denominations. There are scripture readings, prayers, hymns, sermons and Holy Communion. The meeting is scheduled to last for seventy minutes.

Holy Communion has the same purpose in Mormonism as in other churches, to remember the sacrifice of Christ. Mormons do not believe in transubstantiation (the Catholic belief that the host literally becomes the body of Christ), and as Mormons do not drink alcohol water is used in place of wine. The host is blessed by an elder and brought round to the congregation, who remain in their seats, by deacons (12 years olds) and teachers (14 year olds).

Also on Sundays Mormon churches hold a Sunday School and a Priest/Relief meeting; a member of the faith expects to spend around three hours in church on a Sunday.

Temple worship is very different to ordinary church worship. Mormon Temples are very grand buildings which only Mormons can attend (members of other faiths or no faith are welcomed to church worship), and then only those who have a "Temple recommendation" from their bishop (who certifies that the recommended is baptized and of good faith). Temples are used for special occasions such as baptism of the dead and marriages. There is much teaching which takes place in the Temple, as well.

Baptism of the dead is a ritual unique to the Mormon church. Mormons believe that those who did not accept the true faith (or who died before the Mormon Church was established) during their lifetimes still have a chance to accept it after death. For this reason, Mormons have gathered a huge database of genealogy records: the intention is eventually to have the name of every person who ever lived. These people are then baptized by proxy: a church elder will undergo a full immersion baptism for a dead person, which their spirit can then accept (or not) and so enter the Kingdom of God.

Mormons also perform full immersion baptism for the living, but this takes place in church, not in Temple. The ceremony is followed (usually the next Sunday) by the Gift of the Holy Ghost, a laying on of hands which allows the Holy Ghost to enter the baptized. Baptism for those who are born into the Mormon faith takes place when they are eight years of age: Mormons do not believe that babies have the capacity to tell right from wrong and are therefore free from sin, so do not require baptism. Those who die before that age receive the same spiritual benefits as the baptized.

Blessings

The concept of blessing is a very important one in the Mormon faith. Any man who holds the Melchizedek priesthood may give blessings, whilst any holding the Aaronic priesthood may assist with blessing.

Blessings are given to babies, to those joining the church, to the sick and all those seeking consolation. They are performed by the laying on of hands (in the case of blessings for the sick this may be augmented by the use of consecrated oil). The faithful believe that blessings enable God to speak to the seeker through the words of the priest.

The words of the blessing may direct the seeker to study certain passages of scripture or tell them to take a certain course of action; they can help the seeker to make decisions or to understand their problems more clearly. Although Mormons claim that there have been instances of blessings for the sick that have effected miraculous recoveries this is not their main purpose; the blessing may consist of an instruction to seek medical help for the sickness, or in the case of the dying to surrender to the illness and to go in peace.

As nearly all adult male Mormons hold the Melchizedek priesthood they, as head of the household, can administer blessings to other family members.

Chapter 5: Social Matters

Mormon leaders often issue proclamations on social matters, interpreting the modern world through the holy books. Mormons tend to be socially conservative, and their doctrine lays great stress on loyalty, honesty and the family.

Body piercing and tattoos are frowned on in Mormonism as desecrating the body given by God. They are completely discouraged for men and women are counseled to only have, at most, one piercing in each ear and the rings should be modest. Generally Mormons are encouraged to dress modestly, avoiding revealing or tight clothing. Hygienic practices and the avoidance of extreme haircuts are also seen as desirable.

There are special garments worn by Mormons as a symbol of purity and faith, which are essentially similar to normal underwear except that the bottom part is knee length. This underwear should be worn next to the skin at all times (for women even a brassiere should be worn over the top of it), and should only be removed when it is essential to an activity, for example, for swimming. A Mormon should not look for excuses to remove the garments. The garments should always be white as a symbol of purity; the only exception is made for serving military personnel who are allowed garments which conform to uniform regulations.

Mormons are strongly opposed to gambling in any form, believing that it leads people into other sinful behaviors such as theft. The idea of gaining a large amount of money without effort also goes against the strong work ethic which Mormons are encouraged to adopt. Mormon leaders actively campaign against the building of casinos and the running of state lotteries. All forms of gambling are banned in Utah.

The first Mormons had slightly more relaxed dietary laws than those which obtain today: coffee, tea and alcohol were amongst the provisions on the Great Westward Trek (see **Mormon History**, above) and it is known that Brigham Young chewed tobacco. Wine was used as part of the sacrament, as well. The key rule in early Mormonism was that nothing should be indulged in to excess. In the twentieth century dietary laws, were tightened (communion wine was changed for water in 1906): as part of the respect for the body given by God, alcohol, tobacco in all its forms, tea, coffee and all illegal narcotics are forbidden. There is much debate as to the permissibility of caffeinated soft drinks like Coca Cola.

Joseph Smith preached that animals have souls and that meat should only be eaten to ward off cold or famine, and then only in moderation. However, most Mormons are meat eaters and the church has never taken an official position on vegetarianism.

If a Mormon transgresses the laws on gambling or narcotics, he is not thrown out of the church but cannot hold the priesthood or get a temple recommendation (see **Worship**, above). It is the duty of other Mormons to try and guide those who succumb to temptation back to the church.

Marriage and Sexuality

Marriage in the Mormon faith is seen as eternal: a man and woman are sealed together on earth and will remain so in heaven. Marriage ceremonies take place in the Temple. Divorce is strongly discouraged, and all possible efforts are made by counselors to save failing marriages. However, if a marriage breakdown is irrevocable, divorce and remarriage are possible. For men, because of the tradition of polygamy, this requires no special action as a man is permitted to be "sealed" to more than one woman. A woman must apply for a "cancellation of sealing" from the Temple: this will usually only be granted when she is ready to be sealed to another man.

Mormon attitudes to sex are conservative and lay stress on fidelity and chastity. Adultery is forbidden, as is pre-marital sex. "Deviant" sexual practices such as oral and anal sex are forbidden, even within marriage.

Birth control is permitted within Mormonism, and sex without procreation is seen as a way of reinforcing the bonds between husband and wife. The number of children a Mormon should have is a matter between them and God (though all married couples should have some children if they are able to, and Mormon families tend to be larger than average). It is considered undesirable to avoid having children to advance one's earthly ambitions, for example, to afford a better lifestyle or to finish education.

Homosexuality is seen as a sin by the LDS and is strongly condemned. As sex is only permitted within marriage, all homosexual acts are viewed as a sin against chastity. Mormons do not accept that homosexuality is genetically pre-determined, and many Mormon organizations try to counsel homosexual Mormons "back" to heterosexuality. There are organizations which support gay and lesbian Mormons and lobby for their inclusion in the Church, but it remains officially completely forbidden. In 1985, a breakaway group formed the Restoration Church of Jesus Christ, a Latter Day Saints church which accepts LGBT members.

Chapter 6: Branches of Mormonism

As can be seen from the Mormon History section, above, the Mormon Church has frequently experienced schism as different theologies and leaders have fought for supremacy. Although the Church of Jesus Christ of Latter Day Saints, the branch of Mormonism with its origins first in Joseph Smith and then Brigham Young, remains very much the largest, some other groups have significant congregations.

Community of Christ

The Community of Christ considers itself the true heir of the church established by Joseph Smith: indeed it dates its foundation as April 6th 1830 when Smith began his church. It is the largest Mormon group outside the LDS, with around 250,000 members worldwide.

The Community of Christ was formally established in 1860 under the name of The Church of Jesus Christ of Latter Day Saints, with the word "Reorganized" added to the title in 1872. The current name was chosen in 2001.

The CoC believes that Joseph Smith III, Joseph Smith Jr's son, was the true heir of his father's church, and so since the death of Smith Jr in 1844 they have developed in isolation from the LDS.

Although the CoC retains many structural and theological features of Mormonism (for example the Church is led by a President who has a Council of Apostles), it is strikingly different in some ways.

The most obvious difference is that the Church is very much more liberal than the LDS. It preaches the equality of all persons and rejects the use of scripture to set any group higher than another For this reason women are permitted to hold the priesthood and in the 1980s practicing gays and lesbians were also allowed to do so (this has now been rescinded, but those who were ordained when it was permissible have been allowed to retain their posts).

These liberal policies were not without controversy, and, in the latter part of the 20th century, the Church lost around 10% of its membership who left to form other sects.

The Book of Mormon is not regarded by the CoC as being on an equal level with the Bible as scripture, rather as a confirmation of the Bible's message. Debate as to the historical authenticity of the Book of Mormon is permitted and attempts to have it definitively declared as the true word of God have been rebuffed.

Several of the most important sites of early Mormonism are owned by the CoC, including the Kirtland Temple and a site in Nauvoo.

Other Branches

There are a number of other, smaller, branches of Mormonism. These may be broadly defined as fundamentalist and liberal branches. Those detailed below are the most numerous; there are many other very small groups as well as numbers of Mormons who disagree with the mainstream Church but have not organised into new branches.

Fundamentalist Church of Jesus Christ of Latter-Day Saints

An extremely conservative sect which has around 8000 members. The FLDS has been controversial in its assertion of its property rights over those of individual members.

The FLDS practice polygamy as well as "placed marriage", where the priesthood decides on who should marry whom. This practice has created much controversy, particularly when it has involved the betrothal of young people.

In 2008, an FLDS community near Eldorado in Texas was raided by police, who removed 416 children into care, stating that they were at risk of abuse. This raid was prompted by a telephone call which alleged a fifteen year old girl was being forced into marriage with a forty five year old man. It was subsequently determined that the call was a hoax and the children were returned. However, allegations of sexual abuse and marriage of underage girls have dogged the church, and, in 2011, its former President Warren Jeffs was convicted of sexual assault on children.

Apostolic United Brethren

The AUB comprises around 9000 members. Whilst it does practice polygamy it is more liberal than some other fundamentalist groups: it does not arrange marriages against the will of the parties involved, permit marriages between relatives or allow polygamy for under-18s.

The Latter Day Church of Christ (Kingston Group)

The Kingston group originated from the family of Charles Kingston, who was excommunicated from the LDS in the 1920s for refusing to renounce polygamy. His son Elden Kingston declared in 1941 that he had been given a vision by an angel to set up a trading co-operative. This co-operative is now worth over $150M.

This group has around 3,500 members and is extremely controversial for its policies of polygamy, marriage of young girls and particularly for allowing incestuous marriages, which they claim are necessary to maintain the purity of their bloodlines, which they claim can be traced back to Jesus.

Centennial Park Group

A breakaway group from the FLDS located in Centennial Park, Arizona, the CPG are also known as The Work of Jesus Christ. The group split from the FLDS in 1986 in protest at the decision of the FLDS to accept one man rule, rather than rule by a council of priests.

The CPG is somewhat more liberal than the FLDS, although they do practice arranged marriage.

Blackmore Group

The Blackmore Group is led by Winston Blackmore, who was excommunicated from the FLDS by Warren Jeffs for doubting Jeffs' leadership and his claims to prophetic vision. Based in British Columbia, it has around 700 followers. Blackmore has married twenty five times and has over a hundred children: he was charged with polygamy in 2009.

Liberal Branch

It should be noted that there are far fewer liberal offshoots of Mormonism than fundamentalist ones. This is because mainstream Mormonism is very strict in its doctrine, which does not lend itself to adaptation. Those who leave the LDS tend to either join other already established religions or have no religion at all. Other liberal elements have stayed within the LDS and have worked explicitly to liberalise the Church or quietly chosen to drop some of the more fundamentalist aspects of doctrine from their own practice.

The Restoration Church of Jesus Christ

The RCJC was formed in 1985 under the leadership of Antonio Feliz, a bishop of the LDS who had been expelled for homosexual acts. The group had around five hundred members and followed many elements of mainstream Mormon practice, but allowed women to join the priesthood and recognised homosexual marriage, including polygamous marriage.

The RCJC dissolved itself in 2010 after political infighting; it re-emerged as two separate groups, the Reformation Church of Christ and the Church of Christ – Community of the Latter Day Saints.

Chapter 7: Controversies

The Mormon movement has been beset with controversy from its inception, and still is today, although in many instances the cause of controversy has been amended or removed.

Violence

The LDS has a history of using violence in its defence: Joseph Smith was said to abhor violence but when the attacks on the Church from outsiders became intolerable he found it necessary to authorise and in some cases lead paramilitary activity.

In the Utah War of 1857 Mormons fought against the US Government, and in the Mountain Meadows massacre (see **History**, above) committed the most notorious act of violence by members of the LDS.

In 1927, the Church authorities took steps to reform the LDS approach to violence by introducing a Good Neighbor Policy. Under this policy, the Oath of Vengance was removed from the Temple Endowment Ceremony (the welcoming of new members into the priesthood). Previously all priests had to swear that they would seek vengeance for the deaths of Joseph and Hyrum Smith and other wrongs done by the US Government to Mormons.

Race

The LDS has a long and complicated history in its relations with African Americans and other ethnic groups.

The Book of Mormon describes God cursing the Lamanites (the opponents of Moroni's tribe, the Nephites) with black skin, which would make them "loathsome" and mark them out to make sure that the (white) Nephites did not breed with them. However, in other parts of the Book there are admonitions against discriminating between peoples on the grounds of colour.

Joseph Smith originally did not oppose slavery, saying that it was ordained in the Bible that some should be servants and some masters. However, towards the end of his life he became increasingly abolitionist, making it a central part of his 1844 presidential campaign. He also stated that blacks were as good as whites, which was not a view universally held even amongst abolitionists. Several black men attained the priesthood in Smith's time.

Brigham Young had a far less liberal attitude to racial questions. He stated that black skin and African features were the mark of Cain, placed there by God as a punishment. He also said that, after the flood, God cursed black people again, to make them always slaves. Young was scandalized by the marriage of Enoch Lewis, a black Mormon, to a white woman in 1847 and their having a mixed-race child. He quickly banned all black people from attaining the priesthood.

This ban remained, although the subject of much debate, until 1978. During that time, black people could be Mormons, but they were excluded from the main benefits of the religion such as the priesthood and Temple marriage. As opposition grew to the policy, particularly during the civil rights era, Mormon leaders insisted that although the policy would one day change it could not without a divine revelation which had not yet arrived. Finally, in 1978, the President and Council announced the revelation had come (though critics pointed out that it had finally come just as the Church was about to open a large Temple in Brazil, where the exclusion of black people would have been almost impossible).

There are now well over 500,000 black members of the LDS.

Polygamy

Polygamy, or the practice of allowing a man to take more than one wife, is probably one of the main things generally associated with the LDS and the practice which has caused most controversy and friction with those outside the Church.

Polygamy had its origins in the command in the Book of Mormon that a man should "raise up his seed unto God", i.e. worship God by having as many children as possible: clearly the more wives a man had the more children he could provide.

Joseph Smith claimed to have had divine revelations authorising polygamy and practised it himself, though keeping it secret from the wider Church and explicitly stating that monogamy was correct.

Brigham Young made polygamy the common practice of the LDS, and had fifty-one wives himself. This public espousal of polygamy led to direct conflict with the US Government on many occasions and delayed the entry of Utah into the Union for many years. The government passed several laws specifically aimed at polygamy, including a law in 1887 allowing the seizure of Church property due to its polygamous practices. With the existence of the LDS under threat, President Woodruff announced that he had received a revelation that the LDS should cease polygamous marriages. Some Mormons continued to practise polygamy, but it was completely and decisively banned in 1904.

Although it is now banned the LDS still remains faithful to the idea of polygamy, stating that it will exist in heaven, and maintaining its traditions: for example, a man receiving a divorce and remarrying does not have to be "unsealed" from his first marriage as a woman does, as multiple wives are allowed for men. LDS has not definitively ruled out a return to polygamy in the future.

Conclusion

The story of Mormonism is one of the most remarkable in any sphere, in any country, in the last two centuries. For a new religious order to arise from the vision of one man to become a worldwide order with over fourteen million adherents, effectively controlling a whole state of the USA, is almost without precedent in modern times.

The faithful will point to this success as indicative of the truth of their cause and the strength of God's blessing upon them. Those outside the Church must look to a number of factors in analysing its success. There is no doubt that nineteenth century in America was fertile ground for the foundation of new religious orders as the people of a new country searched for their own forms of worship (the equally numerous Seventh Day Adventists, for example, were also established in this period).

The nature of the geography of the United States at the time must also be taken into account. It is hard to envisage any place in the crowded modern world where the followers of a new religion would be able to found their own new city, not once but several times as the LDS did. The establishment of the Church in Salt Lake City allowed it to become numerous and powerful with hardly any outside interference; by the time Utah became a state in 1896 Mormon dominance in the area was fully established.

Throughout the 20th and 21st centuries, Mormonism has continued to flourish. It has at times been beset with controversies, particularly over race and polygamy, but these have not significantly hampered the growth of the Church. Many events, such as the award of the 2002 Winter Olympics to Salt Lake City and the emergence of Mitt Romney as a frontrunner for the 2012 Republican Presidential nomination, show how accepted Mormonism has become in the mainstream of US and global culture (though, typically, neither of these examples are without controversy).

The Church of Jesus Christ of Latter-Day Saints is still growing at a very rapid rate and has become a major lobbying organisation on issues such as assisted suicide and homosexual marriage (both of which it opposes). There is every indication that it will continue to spread and remain a major feature of the religious and cultural landscape both in the USA and other countries for the foreseeable future.

About the Publisher

BookCaps™ is building a library of low cost study guides; if you enjoyed this book, look for other books in the "Plain and Simple English" series at **www.bookcaps.com**.

Cover image © Kalani - Fotolia.com.

Made in the USA
Columbia, SC
15 July 2018